MW00897327

SALES

EXACTLY How To Stop Being a Little BITCH and SELL ANYTHING in 5 EASY Steps

Dan Goldberg

Copyright

Table of Contents

INTRODUCTION

I want to start by congratulating you. You have taken the first step in NOT being a little bitch. You're about to take a huge step in increasing your sales.

Do you want to be able to sell anything, but you're worried that you may not succeed? Do you want to know exactly how the experts do it? You picked up the perfect book! This book contains proven steps and strategies on how to sell anything successfully by just following 5 simple steps.

You will learn 5 detailed steps on how you can prepare yourself, master your product, know your client, develop your own sales strategies, and master the tricks of the trade. You will also learn about the underlying psychological concepts that surround people's communication and buying behaviors. This book will give you a fresh look at how sales should be done!

Thanks again for downloading this book, I hope you enjoy it!

Dan

Step #1: Be Someone You'd Like to Buy From

Sales people are probably some of the most stereotyped bunch. On the positive side, they are usually the ones who are friendly, who think positive, who know their way with words, who dress well, and who reel in the most money, come high school reunion. On the other hand, they are also stereotyped as the ones who are boastful, big-mouthed, and relentless deceivers who will say anything just to sell you something. You bought this book because you want to become successful in sales, but are you willing to fall within those stereotypes?

The answer is easy, of course you wouldn't, and you SHOULDN'T. The first mistake that aspiring sales people commit is that they work from these stereotypes. They center their training on what to imitate and what to avoid, instead of forming their own sales persona. Perhaps the question should be re-phrased into something like, "What type of sales person do you want to be?" Stereotypes cannot be changed, because it will depend on the perception of other people.

If you want to become successful in this area, the best way to stand out is to be someone that you yourself will buy from. Will you buy something from someone who is too friendly and too positive, but also flashy and honey-tongued? If not, then who will you buy from? That's the first question you need to answer in your sales training.

Set the Right Attitude

As the title of this book said, STOP BEING A LITTLE BITCH.

What does it mean? It is about setting the right attitude - that is forming the right mindset to get yourself to act reasonably in any given situation. Let's do little quiz. Picture yourself in the following situations and choose a behaviour that is closest to what you will do:

1. A client tells you to meet at a certain place. Being a good salesperson that you are, you arrived an hour before the schedule. After an hour and a half, you received a call from your client. She cannot make it because "something came up". What will be your immediate reaction?

a) Sigh heavily on the phone and mutter disappointment (and some spells to turn your client to stone)

b) Hang up the phone and walk out of the place, fuming

c) Say that you were waiting and ask how long it will take for her to take care of her business, because you can wait a little longer, or you can re-schedule.

2. You have a product demonstration and you were doing great. In the middle of your demo, the product somehow stopped working. You tried to fix it but to no avail. What will you do?

a) Tell your client you were given a trial product, then call your technical support team immediately and lash out at them.

b) Close your eyes, take a deep breath then hope that when you wake up, it was only just a dream.

c) Explain to your client the possible causes of the malfunction.

3. One of your clients seems eager to buy your product, so you do

your best to give them all the information they need. Time after time, this client will tell you that he is still thinking it over, but he thinks your product is really good. You've invested a good deal of time meeting up with him. Until one day, he disappeared. He changed his number and left his apartment. You found out he retired in a different country. How will you react?

a) You'll track him down and send him hate mails.

b) You'll pretend you never knew him.

c) You'll accept that this happens every now and then, you'll find a new prospect tomorrow, no biggie.

If you answered A to all three, you're a little bitch. You react negatively in situations and you act impulsively. If you answered B to all of them, you're an escapist. Instead of thinking of ways to make the situation better, you escape confrontation or pretend that nothing bad really happened. If you answered C to these situations, then you are reasonable. You understand that there are reasons behind unfortunate circumstance, and you act positively to find an agreement or a resolution.

There is no need to become overly positive to the point that you are no longer thinking realistically. Negative things DO happen. There are clients who do not know how to give early notices, sample products will sometimes fail at the most crucial of times, and there are people who will lead you on to nothing. There is no point denying that life is full of trials and disappointments. The only thing you have to remember is that the way those obstacles affect you is entirely your choice: you can choose to give up, or move on.

Having the right attitude means knowing when it is reasonable to think and act a certain way. Here are some of the things that you can do to make sure that you are not acting out of impulse:

Put yourself in other people's shoes –

If you are the one who made the mistake, how would you feel if someone reacts negatively against you? Do you think that there's a better way to react? It would be easier for you to analyze the situation if you consider other people's feelings and way of thinking. Remember that what you do and say will always have an effect. If you are on the other end of the line, think of the things that you do not want to hear and expect that other people will feel the same way.

Do not play the blame game –

Your clients will be looking at you as if you represent everything that your product is, so take ownership and accountability. It would not do you good to let your clients feel that someone else is accountable for a mistake because for them, it is only you. If you try to put the blame on another person, your clients may feel that you are leaving them hanging with the hopes that the issue will be resolved by people that they don't know.

Explain, do not make excuses –

Do you appreciate it when someone gives you lame excuses? Of course not, so refrain from doing it. Instead of making up excuses to somehow justify a malfunction, explain what is going on and what can be done to fix it. You can only do this if you know your product inside out. In the next chapter, you will learn ways on how you can master your product.

Know that there's always a deal to score –

A reasonable person looks at things like this: It's always possible to have a win-win situation. It is different from being overly optimistic, because you do not expect things to always turn out in your favor. A reasonable person recognizes the possibility to come to a better agreement. To become reasonable, you have to acknowledge that a better deal will have some compromise, but it is a compromise that should be okay for both parties.

You cannot force people to buy –

You can convince them, you can sway them, and you can get them to think highly of you and your product, but at the end of the day, it is their choice. You cannot force people to buy from you. There are some illusions that can be used to illicit a sense of urgency, but you can never shove anything to your client's faces.

Have you ever been to a store where a staff follows you around to make suggestions? You don't like that, do you? It seems like they are pressuring you to buy in that store, even if you're actually just looking around. Do not be that type of sales agent. You should always recognize that people have the power to choose.

If you would like to succeed in the field of sales, set an attitude that you would love in a salesperson. Do not be that woman who confuses you with jargon, or that one who seems to disappear after you made your purchase. Be reliable, reasonable and accountable.

Aim to leave good impressions –

People are judgmental, that's why first impressions last. Your clients will have a mental judgment of you the moment they first lay their eyes on you. They will then have these judgments confirmed or disproved during the first few minutes that they talk to you. That's why it is crucial to make excellent impressions within the first hour of you meeting with your client. There are three major aspects of yourself that you would have to work on: your appearance, communication skills and confidence.

Dress Accordingly –

Your clients' first assessment of your product will be based on what they see in you. A part of human instinct is ocular observation: sizing up the competition, judging feasibility of a habitat, and forming attraction or aversion by visual appeal. The way you will dress yourself is a reflection of how your product is represented. It is essential to know how to dress according to what your product represents.

There is no need for a suit and tie if you're selling home cleaning agents. You will not sell any prime real estate properties, if you dress like a high-schooler. Dressing expensively is not a pre-requisite to becoming successful in sales; it is dressing according to your product and the place where you'll sell it.

Hone your communication skills –

Next, you need to learn how to communicate effectively. You need to sell your product correctly by using the right communication techniques. Here are some of the things that you can take note of:

1. *Say it simply* – Avoid jargon and too much fluff. When it comes to selling a product or an idea, it all boils down to one thing: Does your client understand how it works? When talking about your product, keep your sentences short and simple. Pause every now

and then to give your clients some time to process the information you gave them.

2. *Say it clearly* – It is important that your clients understand every single word that you say, so make sure that you enunciate your words. Do not make any shortcuts or slang and do not assume that your clients will relate to your urban dictionary. To be safe, use words properly without shortening them, like "going to" instead of "gonna" and "want to" instead of 'wanna". You can use these words if you have already formed some level of closeness to your clients, but never do this on your first meeting.

3. *Say it creatively* – You would like to catch your client's attention and hold it for as long as you could, so be creative on your first product presentation. First, tell a story. Stories make people think of actual visual representations of things, so they will be able to remember what you're saying because it went through an elaborate process in their brains.

After getting their attention, state the facts about your product. Then, end it with the best part that you would like them to remember. People's brains are only going to remember the first and last things that were said to them, so make sure that you tell them about the advantages of buying the product in the last part of your presentation. Do not worry about the things in between that they may not remember. It is likely that they will ask you about it or just go to your website for details.

Those are the techniques that you can use when trying to make a good impression. Remember that it is not just about the things that you say, it is also about how you say it.

Be confident –

Another factor that affects people's perception of others is the way that they handle themselves. Even if you dress appropriately and speak effectively, if you do not exude confidence, your clients will doubt you and your product. Represent your product in a way that you want to be represented.

There are many ways to boost your confidence, but in sales, nothing does it better than product knowledge. In the next chapter, you will learn the next step: product mastery.

Step #2: Master your Product

If you would like to be an effective salesperson, the next step that you should do is to study every aspect of your product. The company you're working for or your concept and manufacturing team may give you some materials to work with, but it isn't enough. You have to make sure that you know your product inside out. You cannot expect people to trust you if you do not know what you're talking about. Here are the things that you should know about your product:

What is your product's purpose? – Do you know the history behind the product's creation? Do you know which problems your product intends to resolve? Do not attempt to make a sales pitch if you do not know these things. If you need to ask different people from your company, do so. Don't ever assume that your product training is enough to help you make a sale.

What are the benefits of having your product? – Whatever it is that you are trying to sell, it's there because there is a problem. It is supposed to add value to people's lives. You have to know how your clients will benefit from buying your product.

What makes it different from other brands? – Another way to master your product is to know how it fares with its competition. Is your product better? In what way? You have to arm yourself with this knowledge because your client will definitely ask you about it.

Does your product have flaws? – Sales people are stereotyped as deceivers because they claim that their product is perfect to the bone. You wouldn't want to be that person. You will not tell your clients about the flaws, of course, but make sure that you have an answer when they ask you about it.

There are plenty of ways to know your product. Here are some of them:

Read all the promotional materials first – The brochures and other printed advertisements will give you a good glimpse of what your product looks like from the public's point of view. You will know how your company generally wants the product to be represented. It is also a good way of determining which type of information is withheld from the general public and is exclusive to some clients.

Scrutinize the manuals – If your product comes with a manual, it will do you good to read it thoroughly. You can use it to re-assure your clients that if they cannot find any support, the manual can answer their questions. You also need to check on things that are not in the manual, so you can provide that information to your client.

Ask about common issues – If your company has a support center, ask the staff for the most commonly reported issues. If there's a website where consumers can post complaints, read up on the FAQs and usual concerns. Knowing these, and the actions done to resolve them will get you ready for your sales pitch.

Use your product – The best way to learn about your product's benefits and flaws is by using it yourself. It will not only help you master your product; it will also boost your confidence when presenting it to your clients, because you experienced using it yourself.

Mastering your product is the best way to get your client's trust. You will be using your product knowledge when employing various sales strategies with your clients.

Step #3: Know Your Market and Your Client

Do you know why it is so hard for real estate agents in malls to make a sale? It is because their post is stationary and they do not have any idea who they're handing their brochures to. Most of them would be stationed in booths and they hand out brochures to anyone passing by. In many occasions, they would mutter something that resembles "We have prime locations available, would you like to check it out?" People will either just pass them by or just shake their head furiously. Why, do you think, this happens?

Familiarity is a social concept that strongly affects how people behave and make decisions. The reason why the saleslady in the mall doesn't score a sale is because her prospects are people she knew nothing about. She is not familiar with the people in the mall and they are not familiar with her either, so why would they talk to her? In the same way, she doesn't even know if these people like to buy properties at all. It is that gap that decreases her chances in successfully selling her product.

In sales, it is essential to know your target market. Handing out brochures and talking to random people may get you some sales, but that would take a long time. If you want to be able to sell anything, you need to have a good idea of who you are selling it to. First, you have to know the difference between your target market and your prospective clients:

Target Market – This is the group of people who directly benefit from your product. They are identified by a certain demographic. This means that they belong to an age group, sex, or industry.

Prospect Clients – These are the specific people that you present your product to. They may or may not belong to your target market. Prospect clients do not only include individuals who will buy your product; these also include distributors, investors and retailers.

Selling to the target market is done by advertising. It would ensure a farther reach and it is cheaper than talking one-on-one to each person who belongs to that group. As a salesperson, you will be selling your product to prospect clients. This is why you should already have an idea of who your target market is. These are the things that you need to know about your prospect clients:

Their Needs – Before meeting with a prospect client, you have to do your homework and try to learn things about them. Do they belong to your target market? If so, then it's easy, because it means that they need your product as a solution to their problem. How about investors? Do you think they have the same needs as your target market? Of course not. This is the reason why you need to know the role that your clients play in the industry. Are they consumers, distributors, or financiers?

One way to know what your client needs is to ask about their past experiences regarding similar products. Ask them which products they've tried in the past and the reason why they stopped using, distributing or investing on your products. Clients do not end contracts because the product doesn't give them what they want. They end contracts because the product doesn't give them what they need. They will not give you the details, so you have to learn how to read between the lines.

Their Wants – These are the things that your clients would be glad to have with when handling or using your product. These are the bonuses, the extras, the *more* in "Wait, there's MORE!". Although not as strong in affecting your client's decision as their needs, wants can make them prefer a brand over another.

There are two ways to determine what your client wants. One is by asking them directly. Being straightforward makes sure that you do not make any false assumptions. If your client doesn't seem to know what they want, another way is to get a deeper understanding of their personality. This means that you have to meet with and talk to them several times.

Their Priorities — Out of the things that your clients need and want, some will rank higher in their set of priorities than others. It is important for you to know which qualities of the product they value more than others because in reality, a single product can't have it all. Knowing your clients' priorities will help you in laying out their options.

After familiarizing yourself with your clients' needs, wants and priorities, it is time to develop different sales strategies. In the next chapter, you will learn how to develop your strategies based on the fundamental process surrounding the process of selling.

Step #4: Develop your Own Set of Sales Strategies

Every client is unique, and so you shouldn't really have a template technique to deal with them. Yes, there are general reactions to specific sales strategies, but as humans who recognize their power of choice, your clients may deviate from what's usual. As discussed in the first chapter, you have to have your own style of selling. Whatever your chosen style is, it should be within a specific succession:

Because you are just beginning to decide on your style, here are some of the most effective strategies used by successful sales people worldwide. Look at each one and see which ones you can employ. Feel free to mix and match, as your strategy depends on your personality and your client's needs and wants.

Catching their Attention:

Tell an interesting story –

People love stories. It is human instinct to listen to anyone who tells a story because people expect that they will learn something new. In the early days of human civilizations, storytelling is the only source of new information about food, shelter and danger. No matter how busy a person thinks he or she is, if someone suddenly tells a story, he or she is bound to listen. The moment a person starts listening, various parts of the brain light up to form scenarios.

As a result of this process, people will tend to remember what is being said. If you want to catch your client's attention, start with an interesting story about your product. This is the part where you can use your experience when testing the product and the product's history.

Draw attention to your face –

There are two reasons why this is a good attention-grabbing strategy. First, making your clients look at your face more will help them become familiar with you. Several studies show that familiar faces are perceived to be more attractive and trustworthy. When your clients trust you, you are sure to close a deal.

Second, when your clients look at your face, they will see your facial expressions and are likely to agree. This is a psychosocial phenomenon called *mirroring*. If they see you smile, they will smile too. Smiling will make your client's brain release dopamine—the happiness hormone. They will think they are happy because you are talking about a good product, but it was actually their act of smiling that made them happy.

You have to make sure that your face expresses emotions that you would like your client to feel. To draw attention to your face, make sure that your hand stays visible within the upper area of your body. Make hand gestures that draw attention to your face (without literally saying "look at me", of course).

Give a shocking bit of information –

Another strategy to catch your client's attention is by giving them a surprising bit of information like ridiculous claims, unbelievable statistics, or news that is totally unimaginable. Your clients, as your audience, will want to know more about what you said. They will listen intently on what you will say next. Make sure that you have some bits of trivia regarding your product or industry.

Building their Interest and Desire:

Highlight your product's benefits –

Highlight your product's benefits and make sure to say it in a way that your client will know that their needs and wants will be met.

Tell them about specific cases –

Relate a story about some clients. When your clients feel that there are other people who have benefited immensely from your product, they are going to be interested and would want to hear more. Tell a highly relatable story about another client and make sure that your story can be verified. If you can get some testimonies, that would be much better.

Give them options, but limit it to 3 –

Nothing else affects desire better than choices. It can affect it in two ways. When a client is given options, he would weigh his priorities and would think that you are kind enough to recognize his power of choice. That will make him want to choose one of the options, because it will serve as a display of how good he makes his choices. When a client is given too many choices though, he is not likely to buy anything at all. His mind will be overloaded with pros and cons and to prevent it from being stressed, he just gives it up.

Confirming the Validity of their Desire:

Give statistics –

Once you see that your client is starting to express his or her desire to buy your product, confirm that his or her desire is valid, by giving statistics of people who are already using the product. This will re-assure them that they are doing the right thing.

Use 'loss-aversion' to your advantage –

People hate to lose things, so when it looks like your client is already desiring your product, give him scenarios when he already has it. That would validate their desire, because they will picture themselves using the product. Afterwards, mention the things that they will 'lose' if they do not have the product. Chances are, they will prevent it from happening and they will close the deal with you.

Convince Them to Act:

Create a sense of urgency –

Tell them to act fast by giving them 'extras' if they act immediately. For example, you can say "If you buy today, you get a free consultation", or any other extra service that you can offer. They would not want to miss on those things, so they would likely close the deal immediately.

Create a sense of scarcity –

Do not make up numbers and say there are limited stocks, if there's actually enough. You do not want to fall into the 'deceitful salesperson' stereotype, right? You can create a sense of scarcity without lying. Tell them how many people are interested in buying the product and how uncertain it is that the product they want will be available next week.

You are not saying for sure that there are limited stocks, but you are subtly suggesting to them a sense of scarcity. Your clients would not want to give her desired product to someone, so they will likely act immediately.

Close the Deal:

Assure the client of continued relationship –

Give your clients a re-assurance that they will hear from you again. This will let them feel cared for, and you will likely get referrals from them.

Give them possibilities of rewards by relationship selling –

Successful salespeople know the value of relationship selling: It is when you get other clients who are related to your first client. In order to achieve this, give your first client some perks when he refers other clients to you, like discounts or freebies. This is a good way for you to advance your career in sales.

Your strategy will have to be customized depending on your client's personality, needs, and wants.

Step #5: Learn the Tricks

After preparing yourself, mastering your product, knowing your clients and developing your own strategy, it is time for you to learn the tricks of the trade. Here are some of the best sales tricks that you can use to sell anything:

Trick #1: The Midas Touch -

When conversing with your client, touch them subtly on the shoulder. Scientific studies showed that when an individual is touched by another, the brain releases oxytocin, which is the hormone responsible for the feeling of bondage. Even if the person who was touched didn't notice it, he or she will feel "attached" to the person who touched him or her. Your client will trust you more if he feels the same attachment. Be subtle and do not overdo it though, because instead of feeling attached, your client may feel awkward.

Trick #2: The Anchoring Effect -

People's brains tend to anchor on a given number. For example, if you tell someone that it takes 600 gallons of water to produce a specific drink, then you ask how much it would cost, that person would likely give you an amount within the $500-$700 range. That's because the brain "anchored" on the first number provided. When striking a bargain, give a number slightly above the range that favors you. If you want to sell a pen for $3 dollars, tell your client you want to sell it for $5. You will get $3 at least and $6 at most.

Trick #3: Mirroring -

You can get your clients to agree with your terms by using the mirroring phenomenon. When having a conversation with your client, nod. The nodding action will be mirrored by your client. Their brains will then think that their behaviour is a result of them agreeing with you, so they will agree with you.

Trick #4: The Foot-in-the-door -

The foot-in-the-door technique is one of the most used sales tricks in the world. It involves making a small request that can easily be granted. Psychologists found that people who grant the small request are likely to grant a bigger request made by the same person. Human brains do not like inconsistency, so they make the same decision, especially if the first request didn't do any harm. Make a small request from your client or sell them something really cheap before asking them to buy your product.

Before trying out these tricks to your clients, practice by selling ideas to your friends and family first. You will see how effective these tricks are, as these were based on the general psychosocial behaviours observed by scientists on people.

CONCLUSION

Thank you again for purchasing this book!

I hope this book was able to help you learn the right attitude, how to learn about the product you're planning to sell, things to know about your client, and the tricks that successful salespeople use to sell anything.

The next step is to get out there and test what you learned in the real world! Go and close your first deal!

Finally, if you enjoyed this book, then I'd like to ask you for a favor, would you be kind enough to leave a review for this book on Amazon? It'd be greatly appreciated!

Thank you and good luck!

Dan

More Best Selling Titles for You...

The Sales Series: How to Make More Money in Sales Guaranteed (3 Titles in 1)

1. Sales

2. Sales Scripts for the Phone

3. Copywriting

Copywriting - 5 Easy Steps to Million Dollar Copywriting for Beginners

Preview of What You Will Learn:

1. Steps on how to write catchy titles that will surely capture your reader's attention right from the start...

2. Guidelines on how to write copy with a message that is strongly conveyed and easily understood...

3. Tips on how to formulate content that will surely persuade your readers and further convince them to buy what you're offering...

4. Useful information on writing an effective call to action & close the deal...

5. Finishing touches that make the content more appealing to entice as many readers as possible...

Sales Scripts - 5 Simple Sales Scripts to Sell Anything Over the Phone...

Preview of What You Will Learn:

1. What are Sales Scripts...

2. Basic Principles When Selling Over the Phone...

3. How to Make the BEST Introduction...

4. How to find the Customer's Needs...

5. How to Recommend, Upsell and Get Past Objections...

6. Finally, How to Close EVERY Sale

Made in the USA
Lexington, KY
11 June 2016